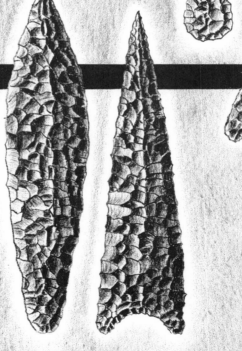

Discovery of metals

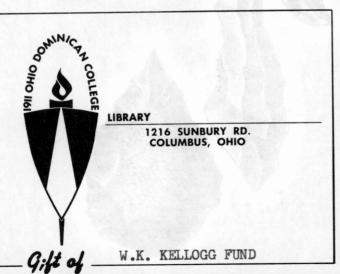

Many people are afraid to admit that man is truly an animal, because they are frightened of wild animals. But men were not always as we see ourselves. Our long-ago ancestors were animals of the wild in every sense that a timber wolf or a baboon is today. They ate what they could dig, pick, catch, and kill. They knew nothing of clothes, or words, or pity. They were stalked and eaten by the lion, just as they stalked and ate any other animal they could outrun, outfight, and out-think. That they quickly learned to out-think all other creatures made them no less wild animals themselves—only smarter.

Our brains, our faces, and our bodies have changed greatly since Dawn Man picked up his first hand-held weapon from a pile of old bones and set out to conquer the world.

World Ecology for Young Readers

HOW MAN BEGAN

written & illustrated by Mel Hunter

WORLD PUBLISHING

TIMES MIRROR
NEW YORK

Published by The World Publishing Company. Published simultaneously in Canada by Nelson, Foster & Scott Ltd. First printing—1972. Copyright © 1972 by Mel Hunter. All rights reserved. Library of Congress catalog card number: 75-184028.   ISBN 0-529-04530-3 (Trade edition); ISBN 0-529-04531-1 (Library edition).   Printed in the United States of America.

For millions of years, man-like creatures have been living on Earth: fighting, learning, dying, but always producing babies whose brains and bodies were just a little bigger and more complex than those of their parents. It seems a vast span of years, but man's entire past history covers only what amounts to the last moment in the story of our planet Earth.

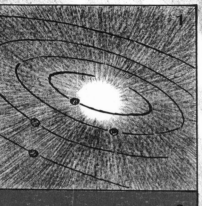

1

Earth and planets formed from dust clouds around sun: 4.5 billion years

First living cells in the sea: 1.6 billion years

First bony animal (worm): 50 million years

First land animal: 250 million years

First dinosaur: 175 million years

First warm-blooded animal: 120 million years

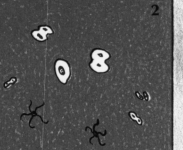

First plants on land: 3
1 billion years

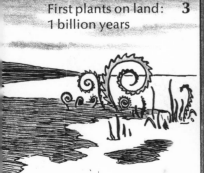

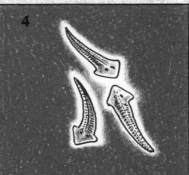
4

5

6

7

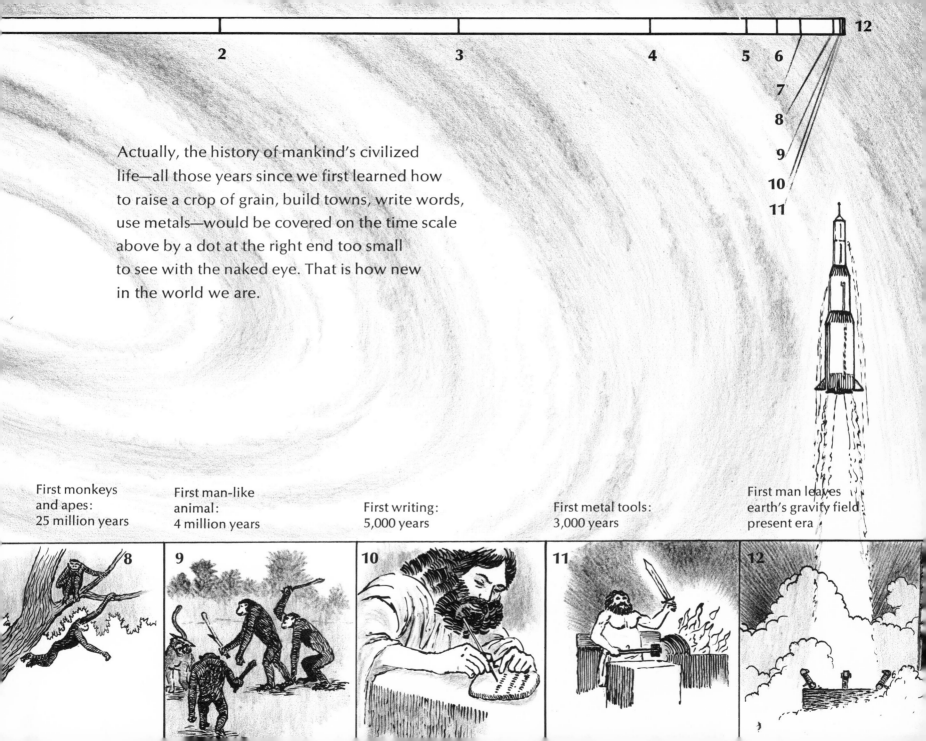

2   **3**   **4**   **5**   **6**   **12**

7

8

9

10

11

Actually, the history of mankind's civilized
life—all those years since we first learned how
to raise a crop of grain, build towns, write words,
use metals—would be covered on the time scale
above by a dot at the right end too small
to see with the naked eye. That is how new
in the world we are.

First monkeys
and apes:
25 million years

First man-like
animal:
4 million years

First writing:
5,000 years

First metal tools:
3,000 years

First man leaves
earth's gravity field:
present era

8

9

10

11

12

Tree shrew

Lemur

Loris

Tarsier

Wild creatures have always faced a terrible struggle to survive: to find food, water, shelter, a mate, a safe place to rear their young. Those who were strong enough or fast enough, or smart enough or lucky enough, survived long enough to produce babies. Some of the babies, would be larger, some smaller, some sharper of eye, some longer-legged. Whichever change worked best for that animal's survival seems to have appeared, in turn, in its own babies. In this way, millions of successive generations of animal babies have gradually produced animals completely different from their ancestors.

There are many ways to diagram animal development, but this one shows how such changes, over millions of years, produced the primate family of animals. Each animal type owes its development to those which came before.

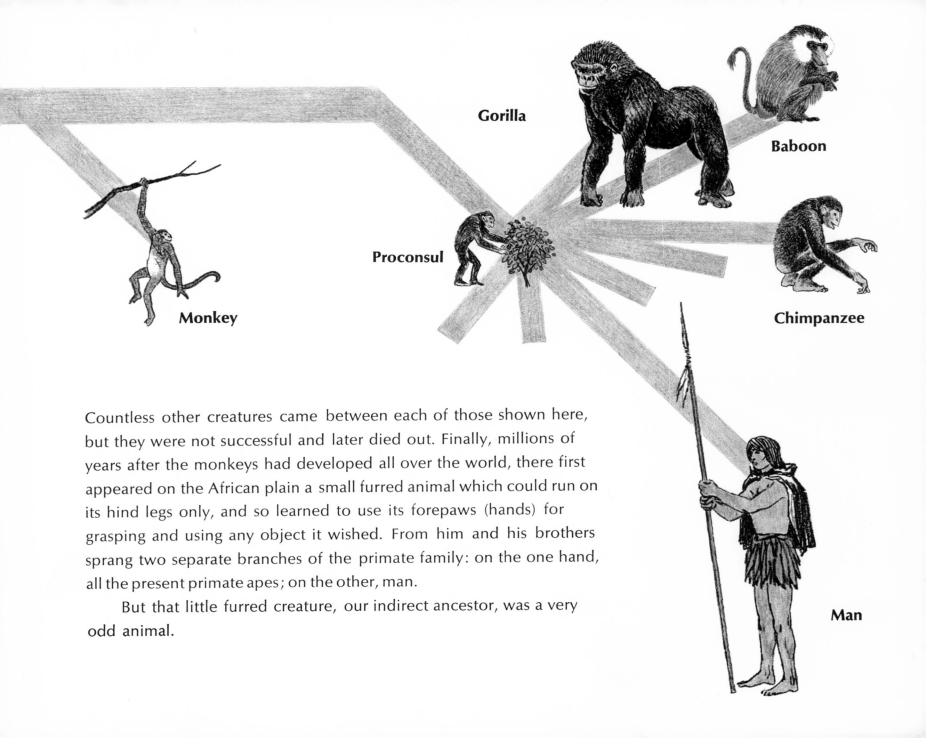

Gorilla

Baboon

Proconsul

Monkey

Chimpanzee

Man

Countless other creatures came between each of those shown here, but they were not successful and later died out. Finally, millions of years after the monkeys had developed all over the world, there first appeared on the African plain a small furred animal which could run on its hind legs only, and so learned to use its forepaws (hands) for grasping and using any object it wished. From him and his brothers sprang two separate branches of the primate family: on the one hand, all the present primate apes; on the other, man.

But that little furred creature, our indirect ancestor, was a very odd animal.

The Proconsul family produced many descendants. One of them combined several unique abilities never before found in one creature. He could run erect on his hind legs with great speed. He could stand tall to see a greater distance. He could use his hands and thumbs effectively. Like other carnivores, he developed stereo vision; whereas most animals have side eyes and poor depth perception.

He lived in large, closely organized groups very like baboons and chimpanzees do today; but unlike them, he learned to eat a little meat rather than lots of plants, and so gained many hours of his waking time for activities other than eating. His large hunting parties, just like a pride of lions today, must have become the terror of the plains.

In the terrible dry ages that followed, he survived on the parched desert grasslands of Africa by killing animals for food, while the plant-eating descendants of Proconsul crouched in the dwindling forests, unable to adapt to rapid changes as he could. His big brain grew rapidly larger.

This was "Dawn Man"—*Africanus*—and one day he did an extraordinary thing.

One day Dawn Man realized that, with his grasping hand, he could grip and swing a club with great force, and so kill a large animal by crushing its skull from a distance, and thus be safer from the teeth and claws of his adversary. It was a great discovery, and almost at once it made little Dawn Man the king of the world.

He learned to collect the shinbones of antelopes. As natural weapons, they fitted into his hands perfectly. He seems also to have collected and split the lower jaws of antelopes, for use as perfect natural cutting tools with which to skin and carve his prey when the hunt was over. With experience, his growing brain was learning to make what he needed.

Within his tribe, he must have been loyal and loving, as are the present apes, with the whole tribe defending as one man whatever they could take and hold.

And always his brain grew larger.

There descended from Proconsul and his brothers a different man-like animal, the one we call *Robustus,* who was much larger than those descendants of Dawn Man we call *Africanus.* The teeth of *Robustus* indicate that he still ate mainly plants, roots, fruit, berries, and nuts, and possibly a few freshwater shellfish when he could find them. But he had not adapted to killing animals and eating meat.

We do not know whether *Robustus* learned to chip flintstones. We are certain that, while he placidly browsed among the plants, *Africanus* learned to improve his own weapons and tools by chipping stones to a sharp cutting edge.

Somewhere in the unknown history of the struggle for life, *Robustus* lost out. He was no match for little *Africanus* and his stone weapons, who would have found *Robustus* as easy to frighten and kill as any other timid plant-eating animal. Fierce natures and killing instincts come only to meat-eaters; and in the wild, meat-eating animals look upon plant-eating animals only as a potential meal.

After the passage of about a million years, man had grown larger, bigger-brained, and much more widespread across the continents of Earth. On the island of Java and in China, Africa, and Europe, remains of this race of men have been found.

Java Man used primitive stone tools, ate almost anything, and lived a life of constant danger in the swamps and jungles of his world.

Also alive in Java at this time was a race of giant primitive man-like creatures very much like *Robustus*. Fragments of their huge skulls and a few great teeth have been found near the remains of Java Man.

Large cave dwellings of a more advanced Stone Age man were found near Peking (Pekin), China. Now called Pekin Man, he had learned the priceless use of fire. He kept his fires going for lighting his cave, for cooking meat, and for scaring off night-prowling predator animals.

His stone tools were more expertly chipped, and the organized life of his tribes made extended residence in a single home cave possible.

Pekin Man's features were more human-looking, less ape-like than those of his ancestors. Still, he regularly ate the bodies of his own kind who met death. Many broken and deliberately split bones show they were opened for their marrow. Even now, 500 thousand years later, ritual cannibalism is known to exist among some tribes of Stone Age men who still live in isolated places on Earth.

Men of the same type hunted even the largest animals. Their bones have been found in North Africa alongside those of the great mastodon, which weighed more than a modern-day elephant. Such a mammoth kill, which brought food for the tribe for weeks, must have been very dangerous for men armed only with stone-tipped spears and crude stone axes. Close teamwork, the development of gestures and word signals, and great bravery made the man of this epoch, even with his poor weapons, more than a fair match for even such giant animals.

Many thousands of years passed, during which the great sheets of ice we call glaciers spread down from the North over most of Europe, Asia, and North America. One great race of men, called Neanderthal, developed a style of life perfectly suited to the cold climate along the southern fringes of the great glaciers. Cave dwellers and great hunters, they were short, heavy, powerful men with low flattened skulls and heavy ridges over the eyes. Their brains were large and as well-developed as ours. They used animal furs for clothing and produced very good stone tools of all kinds.

Neanderthal Man may or may not have been able to develop a real language. But it is certain that he did have a sense of religion and superstition. He hunted and killed the huge cave-bear, deep in the dark caverns of the European mountains, and then buried the bones within ritual circles of objects precious to the tribe, as if worshiping the courage and fierceness of the dangerous animal he had killed and eaten.

Neanderthal Man was a very advanced and successful race of man, but mystery shrouds his strange disappearance from his cave homes. He came to Europe 130 thousand years ago; then suddenly, 15 thousand years ago, he was gone. Possibly, he could not adapt to the warming climate and great changes that followed the retreat of the last ice sheets northward. Possibly, he was exterminated by the sharper spears of his successor race, Cro-Magnon Man. We may never know the true story.

There are many differences between Neanderthal Man and the race of men who took his place nearly everywhere that men lived in the world some 15,000 years ago. Cro-Magnon Man was much taller and and more like men today in appearance. His skull was arched high and narrow, and there was less bony ridge over his eyes. His weapons and tools were far more advanced, many of them carved from bone.

A fierce warrior-hunter, Cro-Magnon Man may have killed off some tribes of Neanderthal Man. Hunting animals with strong instincts to seize and hold large territories—as we are still—do not tolerate competition for food, shelter, and risk of surprise attack when they can eliminate it instead. Although the restraints of civilization were still very far in the future, Cro-Magnon Man is our nearest relative from the past. Many tribes of Stone Age men who closely resemble him still live around the Earth. His children learned to grow crops, tame and keep animals, and build permanent towns. Thus, he began the rapid development of modern man's civilized world.

And, though our world seems very different from that of Cro-Magnon Man, our basic animal instincts are still the same as his, just as his were the same as those of his earliest ancestor, Dawn Man.

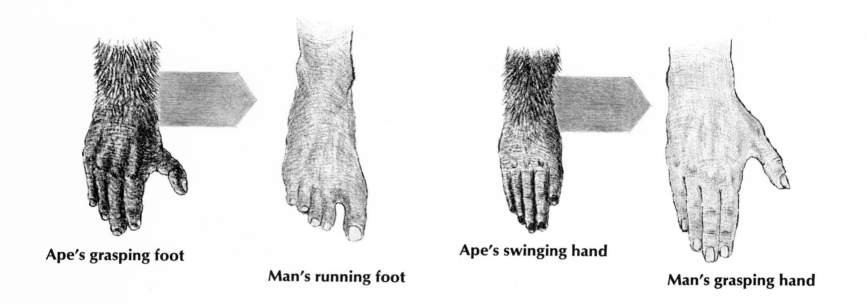

Ape's grasping foot

Man's running foot

Ape's swinging hand

Man's grasping hand

Gradually, on the wide and dangerous plains, little Dawn Man's foot changed its shape from that of the ape who stayed behind in the trees, safe but doomed to remain the same. Dawn Man's hands changed, to grip a weapon rather than a tree limb, and with that weapon he hunted meat. Somehow, too, his enlarging brain learned to look ahead, to plan. It made the vital difference between him and all other creatures.

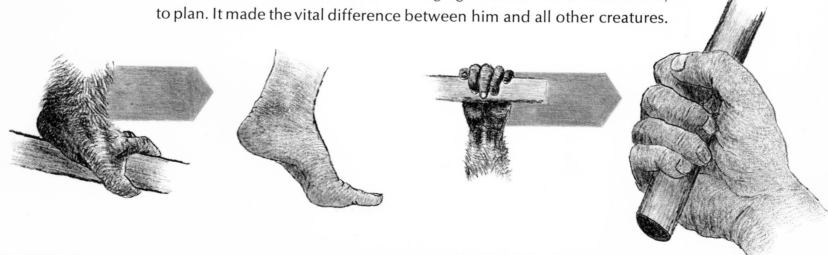

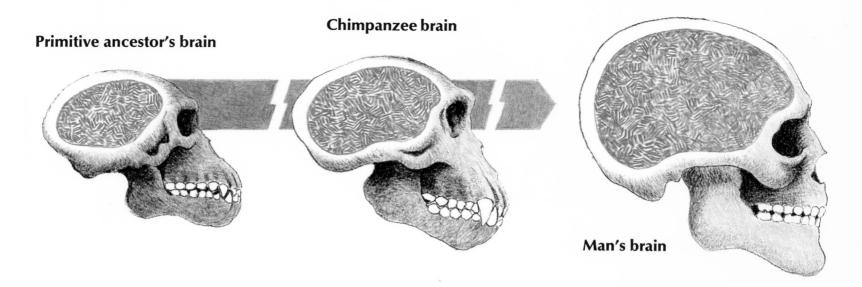

Primitive ancestor's brain

Chimpanzee brain

Man's brain

Today's chimpanzee, with a larger brain, would be no match for little Dawn Man. At a dead end in his own evolution, the chimpanzee cannot plan far ahead and cannot conceive of making a tool. But Dawn Man's fiercest child, modern man, with his huge brain, has progressed from a stone spear to large and complex moon rockets in just a few thousand years. In his brain lies the power to save the natural world from which he has recently come, or to destroy it forever. No one can yet say which he—or we—will do.

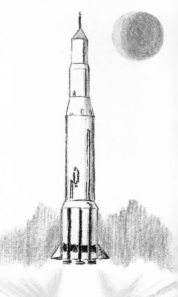

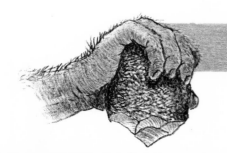

Pre-human animal

**Discovery of stone chipping
for tools and weapons**

Primitive man

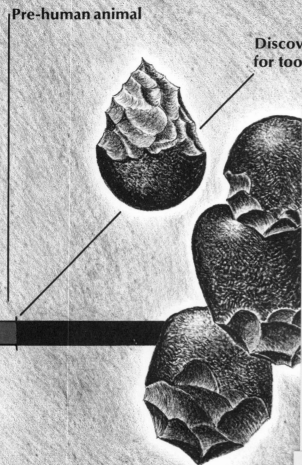